The Rhythm Ain't Gotta Rhyme!

Janet Webb

A Collection of Poetry
Written by Janet Webb

authorHOUSE™

1663 LIBERTY DRIVE, SUITE 200
BLOOMINGTON, INDIANA 47403
(800) 839-8640
WWW.AUTHORHOUSE.COM

First published by AuthorHouse 11/21/05

ISBN: 1-4208-9383-1 (sc)

Library of Congress Control Number: 2005909366

Printed in the United States of America
Bloomington, Indiana

This book is printed on acid-free paper.

Introduction

I remember growing up with the sounds of poetry. The first time I heard the words, "Brown Baby, Brown Baby when you grow up..." I felt that I was that baby, and as I sat in class enthralled while my teacher, Mrs. Vivian Ward Penneymon, read aloud to us in her soft melodious voice the words of Langston Hughes, Paul Lawrence Dunbar, Countee Cullen, Claude McKay, Sterling Brown and so many countless others, I knew in my heart that indeed, "we wear the mask," that there was a reason, "why the caged bird sang."

I knew then as I know now, that one day I would hold the pen and the poetry that is within my heart and soul would be written down to be shared with others. To be read aloud to become a living part of the never-ending rhyme. Enjoy! But remember the rhythm doesn't need to rhyme.

Creativity
flows
from the
ink of
my pen
to the fiber
of this paper
arranging
itself in
words and
phrases
that express
what is me.

Progression of the Rhythms

Self-reflection

The War Within

Do you find, that it's often very hard to reveal the inner
workings of your heart, your mind, your soul?
That it's so very hard to lay bare
Your inner most secrets to all mankind
To rip away the layers of insulation and show yourself
naked to your very core.
Then don't you think it's awful mean, when life plays one of
it's cruelest tricks and determines that life for you is to be a
poet.
It doesn't seem fair to have in your mind an unending chorus
of words,
Rhythms and rhymes
And no matter how hard you try to fight them or how fast you
try to run
Your destiny beckons at each twist and turn
until finally you realize its not a fight you'll win.
So... you surrender, your heart and soul to the pen
You realize... I am what I am...
A poet.
My writing is me...I am my writing
I begin to write with my heart and soul
My private thoughts and feelings all exposed...
My mission is to challenge each of you
To bring forth emotions from deep within
To help you want to laugh
To let you want to cry
To make you want to pray
To challenge you to think
To make you travel along with me
To let you see my life, to live a moment with me
To allow you to become a part of my existence,
Then I become a part of yours...
a memory to cherish, a moment to savior
an afternoon spent with
a poet practicing and sharing her... art...her heart!

The Promise

Made me a promise
when I was real young.
Swore I'd keep it,
it was my major one.
Since then I've struggled hard,
working everyday, to keep that promise
made on that day.
I've kept on struggling; I've kept on striving

to keep my sacred vow.
Knew I'd do it
at times
didn't quite know how.
But through the years
as I've looked back
it was keeping that promise
that kept me on track.
Now when evening time draws nigh
and I settle back...
You'll see no plastic on my dish rack.
No plastic glasses.
No melamine plates.
That's what I promised myself
in this life to have...

<u>No</u> plastic glasses!

<u>No</u> melamine plates!

No Regrets

No regrets,
what I have done is done,
who I am
what I will be, all is done as you can see.

No regrets,
the past is through
today is due
tomorrow unknown
it may not come
Regrets...None

Can I change what's already happened?
Reweave the pattern of life?
I doubt it
Regrets...

Acceptance of the facts
the control is mine,
the choices I made good or bad,
I own them,
they are my own
Regrets...

Spilled milk is spilt
no tears should be shed,
just go back
and milk the cow instead
and fill the cup carefully
the power is yours
to command.
Regrets...none.

What I Chose To Do

It was a deliberate decision
a choice I made consciously,
I chose to teach
that's what I do, teach
that's who I am, a teacher
one who tries to affect and touch the future.
I am a teacher, my subject
is math
through the years my goals were
to add to my students lives – skills and hope and
faith
to subtract from them ignorance, hurt and pain
to multiply their joy of learning,
reduce their feelings of inadequacies
to factor in all that life has in store.
Total this all to prepare a boy to become a man,
Sum up the needs to progress from girl to woman
and do this with
care
compassion
and understanding
that is that.
The simple facts.
I am a teacher, I teach math.

Coming of Age

When does it happen?
Where does it go?
The living of a life for twenty-nine years or so.
When was the day I put my toys away?
How was it done...
this act of magic change?
Am I still the same?
I look in the mirror
what do I see?
An image of myself
as I am
temporarily.
Should I be happy,
angry or sad?
Living a life can't be all bad.
Coming of age
starting anew
each new stage starts out
fresh and true.
A moment of life
an eternity of wonder.
Growing up
or old
or under.

Just Being Me

As a young child
i was content and unconcerned
with my Blackness.
when i got to school
i thought that
in order to prove my
Blackness,
it was necessary for me to
have an attitude of meanness,
that i needed to be hard
and defiant.
As a teen
i thought
that in order to prove my
Blackness,
i needed to defy the
establishment,
to separate myself from
the "man" and all he represents.
As a young women i thought,
that in order
to prove my Blackness,
i needed to be seen at dark places,
doing dark things,
with others
who i thought understood
and acted blacker than me.
It's really sorta sad, when
you think about it
i spent all that time,
energy and effort
to finally realize
what i had intuitively known as a child.
All I need to do ... was to be me.
So I've traveled full circle,
cause now you can
see that
me and my Blackness
have come together comfortably.

7

Self-absorbed

I thought that I had
        gone through some
                stuff in my life.
I thought that I was
        the only one who had
                gone through all the bull...
                        thought I had been the only one to have suffered
                                the only one who had cried
                thought I had been the only one who hurt
                        the only one in pain
                                who suffered in silence
                                cried in the dark
                                hurt in the heart
                                ached in the soul
                                until...
        I opened my eyes
                raised the shutters...
                        looked out and saw all around
                me that I was not the only one
                I was not alone!

To My Mother
(without her I wouldn't exist)

Mom, I can't give you
all the wealth in this land
I can't give you diamonds
or rubies grand
I can't give you all the
time you may want
I can't give you
fancy cars, beautiful houses
or trips abroad.
There are so many things
that I want to give
but
don't have the means.
I don't know if you realize
or even know that there's
one thing I've always given you.
I've given you my love.
Now I may not always
agree with what you
say or do
and
I may not always
do what you want me to do.
But through the years I
always cared about how
you've felt.
And I've tried always
to give you my respect.
I can't always say the
things you want me to.
I can't always do things
the way that you do.
But throughout my life
I've always loved and
respected you.

Now you may wonder why
I wrote this verse.
Well it's just my way
of saying things I've
always felt...and
though I may not show
it by my actions or my words
In my heart I know
you've always had my
love.
So please don't be disappointed
If I do things my way
don't be upset
you raised me to be that way
you taught me to be strong
and the difference in
right and wrong.
You told me to be
my best and on myself
depend.
You taught me
to be independent and
I think I am.
But even though I'm able
to care for myself
I've always realized
I didn't get here by
myself.
You know I've often said
(I don't know if it was to you)
but I've often said,
"I'm glad I wasn't you."
Now
don't get upset keep reading
on.
I'm glad I wasn't you – cause
I wouldn't have
known what to do with
nine hungry mouths to
feed in one house. I've
always believed if I had

been you ~ I'd have packed
my bags and left town
too.
But see, Mom you didn't
and for that I'll always
admire ~ your strength
and faith to remain
beside us.
And as we grew up ~ though
there were many things we
did with out, no one could
ever say that your love
for us ran out.
I'm kinda of sorry that
this took me so long ~ I
should have said this many years ago.
But I've always known it
and so has the man above.
Through it all Mom
I've given you my love.
So sometimes in the evening
as darkness draws near and
you pause to wonder with a
heave and sigh always remember
I love and hold you dear
and though I may not always
say it the way you want me to
or demonstrate it in the things I do.
You've always had my
love and respect.
I owe it to you.

Change

Change
    starting with
      ending up
          change
rearrange
    make different
      other than
         what it was
      or what it will be
          Change
             Change
              Change
make it different
      better than
         tear it down
            to build it
         up throw it
        out make
      room for
    Change
      Change
      empty out   fill it up
      half-way   quarter way
        up,
        up,
        up
    Change what is being done
      to what it will become.

Inspirational

Inspiration

You helped make me who I am,
when you told me what I couldn't do.
When you told me what I couldn't be,
you helped to make me, **me**!
Cause each time I thought about giving up
I remembered you said, "I would",
so of course
I didn't.
Cause why should I prove you right?
You inspired me to achieve,
simply because you didn't believe in me,
or others who looked like me.
But we did and we will continue to succeed.
Not just because of
not just simply in-spite of
no we will continue to succeed
because we carry on the legacy of
our forefathers and mothers
who were great kings, queens, scientists, doctors,
lawyers, singers, dancers, explorers, teachers, preachers,
inventors, laborers, pioneers, butlers, maids, cooks and
nannies, astronomers, astronauts and engineers.
A history that stretches back beyond the pyramids and
continues on and on and on and on
And because I knew who I was,
I knew that no matter what
you thought
or said.
It's what I choose to do
that determines
Who
I
Am.

Mentors

They said that I would never amount to anything.
They said that I'd end up just like all the others.
They said that I would be a burden to my family,
community, state and country.
They said that I didn't have what it took to amount to a
hill of beans.
They said that nothing good ever came out of the projects.
They said you can't give those people nothin'; they don't
appreciate it.
They said well you know it's in their genes...you just can't
expect anything better from those people.
They said this and sooooooo much more, over and over
and over...
until the only good thing about what they said was...
I rarely listened to their words
and for a fact, I never bought their bill of goods;
INSTEAD...
I listen to the voices of the elders who said...
      Child, you can do whatever you want to do.
      Girl, you ain't got to keep on livin' like this.
      Honey, one day you gonna make us all proud.
      Baby, it's not where you come from what matters,
        it's where you ends up that's important!
      Little sister, we expect a lot from you, cause we
        know you can!
I heard those voices say these things and so many more, over
        and over
        and over
        and over
...until I believed in myself that I could.
I hear those voices still, they carry me on now.
And I know I will.
They are my inspiration...
and because of the elders I will continue on,
For now I know....
                I CAN !!!

To Stacie
(AND ALL THE OTHER BLACK CHILDREN GROWING UP IN AMERICA TODAY)

I know your pain
I know your hurt, anger and confusion
I know the look in your eyes, the ache in your heart
I understand.

I know your pain
I've lived your life; I've walked your path
I understand...more probably than you can realize at this time.
I feel the depth of the hurt that threatens to consume you.

I know your pain
Looking in a textbook, expecting to find something, anything about
you, yourself, your past, present and finding nothing.
Listening to the lecturer hoping to hear something about our
struggles, about our pioneers, cowboys, explorers, discoverers,
historians, achievers, makers, molders, anything about those who
look like you and hearing only the silence.

I know your pain
As you strive to achieve in an environment that denies intellect as a
means to anything for a black child. Where it's more important to
possess rhythm or ability to slam- dunk.

I know your pain
I understand the depth of your hurt, as you try to prove your own
self worth.
As you try to work within the system and in doing so not let the
system erase who and what you are.

I know your pain... as did many of those who came before you or I,
could also understand.
I know your pain...but you can't let the pain control your life.
You can't let the pain consume you or define who or what you are.
You must learn to use the pain.

I know your pain...and just as the sword is not done until it
withstands the test of fire,
The wonders of the world were not until they withstood the test of
time
A miracle is nothing until it withstands the test of faith
You will not be...until you withstand this test of pain.

Heroes

Dr. J, Mr. T,
Malcolm X, Mohammed Ali.
Who told you who my heroes should be?
Harriet Tubman or Luther Vandross
heroes can be just plain folks.
Medgar Evers, Martin Luther King, Marcus Garvey,
Crispus Attucks,
Joseph Cinque, Misha Wofford, Aretha Franklin, Byron Hooks
a roll call of black folks,
some not in books!
Malcom X and Huey P
Who told you who my heroes should be?
Mamie Lee Smith, Sojourner Truth, Lynda Watt, Carl Stokes,
Gene Bell, Vivian Penneymon, Helen Cromer Cooper.
Heroes all have their stories to tell.
My heroes
those who I look up to
how dare you try and tell me who they should be.
My role models
those who blazed my trial,
hey, they may not be your heroes as well!
Zan Norwood, Sam Johnson, Elisha McCoy, Granville T. Woods,
Cater Woodson, George Washington Carver, Benjamin Mays.
My heroes
they are mine
they don't have to be yours.
So don't let TV or movies or books or teachers or preachers
decide who your heroes must be.
Take time to find those who provide meaning to your life
and decide all on your own
who your heroes will be.
And when you're done have a roll call of your very own.
For no one, not anyone can tell you who your heroes must be!!!
However...as for me
Dr J., Mr. T.
Malcolm X... Mohammad Ali

Being A Man

All he was trying to do was to be a Man.
Well, not just any old Man but his own Man.
I suppose he never really knew what to expect,
or when to anticipate what might be coming.
His only goal was to be a Man, his own Man.

So many were confused by the way he chose to carry himself,
and by the way he behaved, they weren't quite sure how to
react.
Cause he wasn't at all like anything they had ever seen.
He only wanted to be a Man.

He never fully realized that by being black in America,
his dream would not be made easy.
However, he went on his way,
intent on becoming ... his own Man.

Never letting others decide for him what to do or not to do.
Never worrying about the whispers and looks he received, as
he went about molding his life.
It was almost frightening to watch his development.

Some of them mocked him,
many of them scorned him,
and there were those who chose to try and abuse him.
But none of them ever stopped him.
And even yet today you'll hear people whisper in awe as he
walks by,
there he goes... he is what he always planned to be...
A Man.

Not just any man,
he's a strong, proud, independent, intelligent, loving, caring, God-
fearing, dedicated, determined black man living in America.

He is A MAN!

Rise Above It

Rise above it
the petty comments
raised eyebrows, knowing looks, wicked smiles
snide comments, catty retorts.
Rise above it
Mean spirited remarks, shouted from the dark
Brush-offs, icy glares, ugly stares
Rise above it
Do what you know is right
Rise above it
Smile from your heart not just from your eyes
Be real
Don't act the fool
Turn the other cheek if needed
It doesn't make you meek or weak
Besides your inheritance has already been foretold.
Rise above it
Live your life irregardless of what others think
Carry yourself in a manner such that you don't need to
apologize for
who you are and what you do.
Just keep doing what must be done to carry on.
Rise above it!

Self-discovery

Revolution

What if I
decided
not to let you
determine
what my life will be
what if I
realized
that you don't have
the power
to control
who or
what
I am
what would happen
then?

Determination

I wanted to write a poem but I didn't have a rhyme
I wanted to write a poem but I didn't have the time
I wanted to write a poem but I didn't have a theme
I wanted to write a poem but I didn't have the words
I wanted to write a poem but it had to be one that
nobody else had ever heard
I wanted to write a poem but I didn't know what to say
Yet as you can see a poem was written anyway!
And as I looked back at those lines
A thought ran across my mind
About how many of us want to but don't
Because...because...because

We just don't get it
We just don't understand
That wanting and doing are two separate things...

So unless you want to
Go through life
Wanting and waiting and waiting and wanting
You might try doing
It's amazing what can happen when you do.

The Wish

wanta be
        wanta be me
                wanta know who I am
                        where I'm gonna go
                                who I'm gonna be

wanta be
        wanta be a part of life
                wanta be a living breathing being
                              wanta be loved
                              wanta be cherished
                                  protected
                            sheltered
                            cared for

wanta be
        deep down inside
                wanta be
                        better than what I used to be
                                wiser than I am

wanta know people care
                        truly care about me
                            not what I can do for them or
                                      be for them
                        wanta know they care for me, just as I am

wanta do
        wanta do a whole lot
                wanta make my mark
                        wanta leave some footprints on the sidewalk
wanta know my life was worth living
                        wanta do things that
                                have never been done

      wanta see things in a different way
                wanta learn to love myself
      wanta be important to me
wanta
        wanta be
                wanta be the
                      wanta be the best
                        wanta be the best me
                                just...wanta be

Different Drummer

I've heard that...
they say I dance to the beat of a different
drummer;
they say i step to a tune never heard;
they say i move to a rhythm never played;
they say i move to a beat only i can hear.
They do not recognize that
i dance,
i step,
i move
i live
a life that is not just my own
i dance to the beat of drums played centuries
before
we landed on these shores
i step to a tune sung by kings and queens
i move to a rhythm ingrained in my soul
a beat that pulses as blood through my veins
i am all that was
all that will be
i am
me!

Growing Up (Still not grown)

I have arrived (somewhere)
not at the final stop (perhaps)
of my destination (I think)...
but someplace other than
where I started from.
I have arrived (somewhere)
stepping out upon the stage
spotlighted and highlighted
raised up...set apart...
I have arrived (somewhere)
somewhat afraid of what may (will)
happen this time...yet
still willing to step forward
to try...
I have arrived
somewhat battered, tattered
a little worse for wear
seasoned, honed, fine tuned,
experienced, wiser
yet still starry-eyed, naïve.
I have arrived
at the beginning
of the next stage
of my development,
hopefully equipped
with the skills necessary
to continue on
cause as you can see...
I have arrived.

Journey

I packed my bags (included all my self-respect and my pride)
Cleaned out my room (gathering up all my memories)
Closed the door on my youth.
Loaded all my baggage in the trunk of my ride "Adulthood"
    And then I took a drive
Sign ahead proclaimed…"This way to Growing Up"
Entered on the highway…destination decided, I'm gonna
ride "Adulthood" until I'm all grown up.
Passing by lots of cars traveling the same way –
signal lights,
 switching lanes,
looking for road signs…
there goes one.
 Pre-Teen Age 2 miles straight ahead exit to the right,
then there's exits 361 and 362 a quarter mile,
lets see teenage years and young adulthood exit to the
left – break ahead highway is under repair,
damage caused by sex, dope and drugs
Sign post coming up – marriage booth merge to the right,
pay the toll, pick up some kids if that's your goal
or exit here to the left – speed it up you're on the
express.
Driving down the highway
Searching for a life
Destination - to grow up
Process - to do it right
Please pay close attention
To all signs and signals posted
This is a one way journey,
there's no turning back.
So fasten your seatbelts,
look to left and right
Proceed with caution,
this is your life.

Intracellular
(TRAVAELING WHERE NO OTHER CAN GO)

I lost myself a while ago
I really don't know when.
I ran away from myself
and now I can't come in.

I lost myself in myself
searching for a place to hide.
I hide myself from myself
so well
that now I can't find myself in me.

I lost myself in myself
searching for my soul.
I've forgotten where the search began,
I have no idea where it ends
or if it ever does.

I've lost myself inside myself
and discovered in myself another self
that wants to be me.

Ode to Middle Age

I went to get up the other day
my bones and muscles didn't work the right way
my hips were stiff and sore as were my ankles and my knees
I didn't know why...
I hadn't done nothin' to make them that way
just climbed into bed and went to sleep...
woke up rolled over and yelped in pain...
who stole my body where did it go?
This one can't be mine,
heck it's too old
aches in the shoulders, elbows and thumbs,
arms ain't long enough for me to see to read
I can't believe this is happening to me.
Me, I'm suppose to be the "baby,"
"youngster," "rookie," "the new kid on the block."
Then I made a crucial mistake, I peeked in the mirror,
caught sight of my face,
it's got
crows feet, wrinkles, and liver spots,
streaks of gray runnin amok in my head.
"Owa no," I shouted that lady just can't be me.
She's somebody's mama, grandmamma, she just can't be me.
Cause I'm young and giddy, mischievous, carefree.
My eyesight must really be failing. I know this just can't be.
What happen to time...I just climbed into bed, that's all,
shake me, maybe I'm still asleep.
No...it's not a dream,
I've grown older as it seems...
but don't be confused by the outside view,
cause age is a mindset I might be aging,
but I'm not growing old.
My mind is still nimble, active and clear.
I'm young in my thoughts if not in my years.
So hear, hear's to growing up and not old,
it's not for the faint of heart
at least that's what I've been told.

Recording Live

I'm gonna be the star
of my life show
spotlight shinning
only on me
doing what
being what
I want to be
Enter stage right
cross to center
seek out the bright.
It's my time
to be.
Lights.
Cameras.
Action.
No scripts.
No rehearsals.
No retakes.
No understudies.
No safety nets.
No intermissions.
It's my life...
and
I'm gonna shine!

Multicultural Dialogue/Diversity In Action

I need to be able
to find
the right words
to express
what I feel
in such away
that you will
be able to
understand
what I mean.
And...I will
know that what
I said,
is what
you heard.
And... that what
you
understood
is what I
meant for you to hear.
In that way,
maybe
we can begin to realize
that
what appears to be different
is not really.
And that though
we are not
exactly the same,
we are not so much unalike
that we can't
begin to understand
one another.
And... in understanding,
begin to accept
and celebrate
the fact
that we are
each of us
just what we are.
No more
no less
and in knowing
this
we can.... just be.

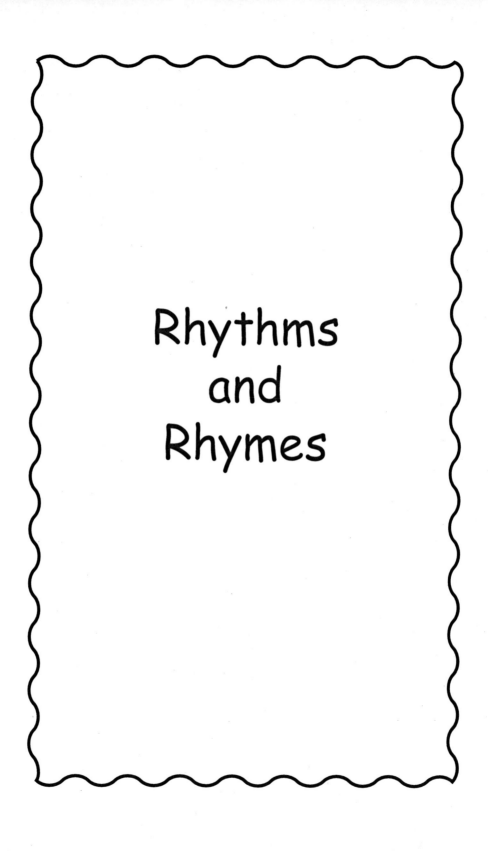

Rhythms
and
Rhymes

Integration

Integration...mixing the essence embodied
in me and you to become
something different other than
me or you
something never seen
yet dreamed of...often
by many
before and now...
hazy, unclear, intended
to happen when you become
more like me...or
I become more like you...or
we become something
more than either of us
alone could be...
so that we
are no longer seen
as us
or them
or those
just seen as human
just seen
not prejudged
just seen...

The Challenge

Why do i need to know this
when am i going to use this
what does this have to do
with who i am
or what i want to be
or what i want to do?
Why do i need to learn this?
What am i going to do with this?
What's going to happen if i don't?

You didn't know this
you didn't need this
so why is this suppose to be important to me?
The world is always changing.
Nothing stays the same.
Nothing's what it was.
Nothing's as it'll be.

So....why do i need to know this?
How am i going to use this?
And what's going to happen if i don't?

Teach Me

TEACH ME, TEACHER, SHOW ME HOW!
TEACH ME, TEACHER, TEACH ME NOW!
SILENCE, CHILD, AND TAKE YOUR SEAT
FOLD YOUR HANDS AND WATCH YOUR FEET.
CHILDREN SHOULD BE SILENT, NICE AND NEAT!
TEACH ME TEACHER, SHOW ME HOW...
YOUR MOMMA SHOULD'VE TAUGHT YOU CHILD.
WHAT DID YOU LEARN LAST YEAR?
MY GOODNESS CHILD WHY ARE YOU EVEN HERE?

TEACH ME TEACHER, TEACH ME NOW...
IF YOU HAVEN'T LEARNED THIS YET...WELL, I DON'T
KNOW WHAT TO SAY, WHY DO YOU COME TO SCHOOL
ANYWAY???
TEACH ME, TEACHER....
I'M LOSING HOPE,
DON'T WANT TO TURN TO DRUGS, CRIME OR DOPE.

TEACH ME TEACHER...
baby here's the way
SHOW ME HOW...
to load and hold a gun
TEACH ME TEACHER...
now say this real clear and loud
TEACH ME NOW...
GIVE ME YOUR MONEY OR I'LL TAKE YOUR LIFE!
I WANT ALL OF WHAT YOU GOT, I WANT IT ALL
RIGHT NOW!!

teach me, teacher
please teach me
<u>now!</u>

Do as I say

Hey world – yea I'm talking to you...
"What's up with this?"
You want me to be
what you choose not to be.
You want me to do
what you yourself don't do.
You want me to act
better than you choose to act.
You want me to wear
stuff you'd never wear.
"What's up with that?"
You want me to walk
down roads you never walked.
You want me to talk in ways
I've never heard you talk.
You want me to respect,
though you never give or show respect.
You want me to be honest, when you seldom tell the truth.
"What's up with that?"
You want me to believe what I know is untrue,
then you look at me cross-eyed and perplexed.
You don't understand why
I am the way I am.
You blame tv...the Hollywood crew.
You blame my teachers, my friends and my schools.
You blame the music, the food that I eat.
"What's up with that?"
Don't you understand for me to do what you demand
would be so much easier if I could follow you.
Cause you should set the example,
you were to blaze the trail.
You should be my role model, whom I'm suppose to look up to
So think...
before you make your demands.
Are you prepared to act
the way you want me to?
If you're not...
"What's up with that?"

The Fight

He said (yes he did!)
cause she said she heard him when he spoke
He said (un, huh) - Yes he did
that she said that
what he said wasn't
what she said,
but then they said
that when he said
what he said
that you said
that no matter what
he said, he couldn't say nothing
cause she said
he can't say nothing
cause we all know that
what you said was the gospel truth.
So then she said
that they said
that it don't
really matter who said what,
cause the
statement done already
been said.
So watch yourself today.
Cause they say that
what was said
done got back to you know who
and
when they find out
what he said to you
when you told him
what they said,
she's gonna be real upset
cause she say
that she never said nothing
no way...and that she ain't
got to say nothing...
cause she's gonna let her fist
do the talking'...so now what you gotta say?   It's on!!

38

Romance

This Is Not A Love Poem

I've never written a love poem,
not really,
you know about feeling all mushy and giddy and happy.
No, I've never written a poem
like that.
Now I've written some stuff
about how many times you done torn my heart out,
walked on it and left me alone.
Then there are the ones about
leaving me for somebody else
and there are always the ones about
one day your gonna get yours,
cause you done, done me wrong for the very last time!
But a love poem,
about holding hands and gazing deep into your eyes, NO!
I ain't never wrote a love poem...wonder why?
Cause I know I've been in love at least a time or two, OK!
(three may four)
A love poem all flowery and sweet. Never!
It seems kinda hard to capture those feelings
and put them down on paper
so that they sound real,
or maybe it's better that no one knows how it really
makes me feel.
Love?
It makes me less defensive,
less aware of, kind of vulnerable, silly!
I just don't want everybody to see how silly
love makes me.
How totally out of control.
So don't go turning pages to find out did she write one
cause as I said,
"I've never written a love poem ever...........................not
really!

The Perfect Rose

He gave me one Perfect Rose.
"Honey is that the best he can do? Cause you coulda bought
that yourself!"
He gave me one Perfect Rose.

"If a man can't bring me at least a dozen and some Korbel,
girl, he can go straight to...!" "Uh, Un, don't say that honey,
he did bring her one, couldn't afford much more than that."
"How many times are you gonna tell us about that funky ole
flower?" "The man gave you a rose, not a diamond!" "Shit, did
he even get a card?" "No, the man's too cheap – he sent her, no
he couldn't afford to send it...so he brought it over in his own
grubby, dirty little hands
a flower, probably half dead." "Girl's don't be so hard on the
man...she said, it was a Perfect Rose."

Let me finish, he gave me...

"If he didn't give you keys to a car, a diamond, new dress, a
night on the town, if he didn't give you anything other than
that damn flower just stop talkin." "Now my Henry, when he
was gone (with his other woman) sent me orchids, yes he did,
orchids." "After John and me fought he sent me to Spain
(yea, girl cause you was in such pain)," "and you've seen these
diamonds on my neck, now that's a gift to talk about! (Sho
nough, one slap per karat)", "So what, your man gave you a
rose!"

Please let me tell you, it really wasn't the Rose so much...

"You mean there was more! Come on girls, listen up!"

Well, you see, he gave me one Perfect Rose that he grew, and
his promise.

"Oh, shit the man done gave her a promise and a home grown

rose. Um uh, what was so important about his promise?"

Well, he promised to treat me like he treated his Roses, he promised to protect me, he told me he would always provide nourishment, warmth and love. He said that like the Roses, our life may have some thorns, but I should always know it would be crowned with his love. He told me that no matter what may happen or how things might change, I could always count on his being there for me. He gave me one Perfect Rose grown with his gentle touch, watered with his love, and nurtured with his tender care.
He gave me a Perfect Rose!
"Damn! Can you believe that, her man gave her a Perfect Rose!"

Reawaken

You have caused me to feel emotions I thought I'd never feel again
You have caused me to see live through the haze of happiness, being carefree...
Just from hearing your voice over the phone
A blast from the past opened up memories that I had long ago packed away
Memories of us in our younger days
Eyes filled with wonder – as we explored, finding out what had often been found out before, yet for us it was all brand new
We were adventurous setting out alone, blazing a trail to sights unknown
The wonder of youth
The thrill of the first
Hearing your voice, brought these sensations back up
The memories of our evenings spent, stealing moments of passion,
hours of content
The twinkle in my eye, was still there, though pressed a bit back
From lives cruel stares,
Yet hearing your voice, feeling its power,
causes a reaction
deep and profound.
What would happen with the stroke of your hand
the brush of your lips
the feel of your hips?
If hearing your voice makes me feel like this
What will happen....when I'm actually with you again?
That's what I want to find out.

Let's Try Again

I know I hurt you,
    but then again
        you know you hurt me too!

I know I disappointed you,
    but then again
        you disappointed me too!
I know I wasn't always just what you wanted me to be
    but then again
        you weren't always what I wanted then.

However, since we have decided to try again
the past is no longer important!!!
Just the knowledge that we are friends
and as this relationship develops
and travels on this course
let's remember
that...
You will be there for me
and that
I'll be there for you.

Because this time around
We won't just be lovers
This time we'll be friends,
True friends until the end.

Judas Still Walks Among Us

She was my friend
and we talked
often
she always listened
she was my friend
our conversations
ranged from current events and fashions
to my personal passions
from interest rates
to intimate dates.
I talked
she listened (carefully).
I told her things
I've never shared with anyone
my quirks, fears and short comings
she didn't judge me
she was my friend
she just listened (very carefully).
When I meet him
the man I just knew
was my Mr. Right
I called and told her about him the very same night.
I told her
everything that happened then
And I told her everything that's happened since.
She listened (real well)
so I told her about what he brought me
(flowers, candy, wine...dresses, shoes, jewelry things so
fine!)
she listen intently
while I told her about the places that we went
(movies, dinner, theatre, sporting events)
she tuned in real close
when I mentioned how much money he always spent
(like helping me with last months rent)

and of course I told her about our fights
and that things just weren't going right.
I talked to her often
almost every night.
So I must admit I was kinda confused and a little
dismayed
when she didn't answer her phone for several days
(My man just happen to be away)
and I just needed to talk
to somebody.
So when she did call me back
I told her about how he had started to cancel plans
that we had made and how sometimes
I didn't see him for several days.
She just grinned a little and replied,
"Well you know, he's just being a man."
She was my friend
and I cried on her shoulder
when I finally realized my Mr. Right was wrong for me
and she was there to listen as I poured out my heart.
She was my friend.
So I'm sure you'll understand
the state of confusion that I'm currently in...
You see the other night I called her house and
he answered her phone . . .
"Hello, I'm sorry my wife's not at home, is there a
message?"
And all that I could think to say was,
"Message...uh tell her I thought she was my friend."

It's Over

Sitting in my lonely room
fighting off darkness and gloom
trying to remember happier times.
Days of laughter, flowers and wine.
Days when I was yours and you were mine.

Trying to answer the questions...
of why?
Why do things have to end this way?

and when.
When did it change between you and me?

and how.
How could this have happen to us?
How did we let it just slip away?

Sitting in my lonely room.
Fighting off the darkness and gloom.
Getting back only more questions from the silence.

Someday, I know I'll break out of this room, filled with
darkness and gloom.
Someday, I'll break from the filling of despair and once
again breathe fresh, crisp, clear air.

As for now...
I'll just sit
and let the darkness comfort me
and the stillness soothe away my pain.

Rejected

Turned me down
put me out
told me
No
you've got to go
Said, "I can't
not today
see ya...maybe
but not today."
So I left
with my head held high
clutching onto my wounded pride.
Not a tear was shed.
Though deep inside
I wanted to cry.
I left your room
without a kiss or a wave
I left with only
this thought...
I know
you'll want me back someday
and when you do
what will I say,
"Rejected Baby...
I can't today
see ya...maybe
But not today."

Closure

I didn't realize it until today
when I saw you with her
the two of you together
with your family
the one I used to dream about having...
with you.
That's when I realized that I no longer
felt the need to be angry or upset or
mad or
bitter or most importantly
sad.
That's when I realized I had forgiven me...
I had forgiven myself
for loving you
when you no longer loved me.
I had forgiven myself for dreaming
that one day
we would have a life together.
I had forgiven myself for all the silly things
I had done
to try and get
then keep your attention.
I had finally forgiven myself.
I had long ago forgiven you...
but I had never moved on.... emotionally.
Last night when I went to sleep
I didn't dream about
what could have been.
I woke up
realizing I had dreamt only about
what was.
At last I know
I've finally let go
and now I'm free
to move on.

Frustrated

Watching you
Unable to help
Seeing you
Hurting
Hurting myself
Unsure what to do
Unsure what to say
Wondering
Do you need me
Watching you
Slowly slipping away
Watching me
Watching you
Not knowing what to do
Wanting to hold you
Yet having to let you go
Seeing me, seeing you
Unable to reach out
Unable to touch you
Mental telepathy
Feeling the same vibes
Drum beat, telephone, telegram, letter
Watching me try to reach you
By any means necessary
Wondering
Do you realize
I share your pain
Don't shut me out
Don't leave me alone
Your hurt
Your pain
Are mine
We are one and the same
So for now
I'll keep watching you...from a distance.

Honoring the

Elders

Crystal Stairs
(A tribute to the man Mr. Langston Hughes)

My momma
she used to read to me
a poem about some crystal stairs.
She used to say to me,
"Child you best take heed,
listen whilst you can,
cause life for you
ain't gonna be sweet.
There'll be no crystal at yo feet.
The stairs you climb,
gonna be concrete.
Dirty
Nasty
Steep
and Deep
with no places to sit
and none to pause,
each ole step,
you gotta walk'em all.
Carrin yo burden
without bowin' yo head.
Clearing a pathway,
makin a mark,
so that others that follow
won't have to travel lost in the dark.
So whilst there's time,
best get you'self ready.
Cause ain't gonna be
no roadmaps,
streets,
nor signs.
You just gotsta find yo stair step
and start yo climb."

Just Here

I'm just here
that's all I am, here.
Now that may not seem like much to you
but to me it's the most important fact.
I'm just here.
No, I'm not doing much of anything you might call
important
Or saying much of anything you might think you want to
hear.
Fact of the matter is...I'm just here.
You should understand though,
that my being here is a statement into and of itself.
Because, I'm still here!
In spite of all you have tried to do to me
and mine
from the time you stole us from the places of our
ancestors
and brought us to these shores
on this land
that is not ours or yours
and here you've tried in vain
to rob us of everything...our spirit, pride, history, identity,
all that we were are...will be.
However, as you can plainly see...
I'm still here!
Maybe not as I was...
certainly, not as I will be.
For I will be
Here!
More determined than ever
to remain and remind you of the past
and to keep watch over you in the future.
For always
I.........WILL........BE.........HERE!

The Request

Mommy, can I take it off today?
Roll it up and put it away?
What, my child, what did you say?
Mommy, can I take it off today, roll it up and put it away,
were prying eyes can't see? Mommy, can I please?
Take off what? Put what away?
My skin, Mommy and my kinky hair.
Can I take them off today? Put them in a box? Tuck
them far far away?
Come here, my child, and hold me close.
Tell me, baby, "Why do you want to hide the beauty of
yourself?"
Mommy, it's like this; at school they look and point and
shout, that ugly black-thing is about. On the news almost
every night, black folks cause all the fuss and fight. I
heard it on the TV and radio too, those black uncivilized
things must go. They bring down our property values,
increase crime, use drugs and dope. Mommy, each and
everyday no matter where I go or what I say, they look
at me with doubt and fear.
Mommy, please can I take it off and put it away? It's not
forever. I swear.
I'll wear it in the house with you.
But, Mommy, please don't make me wear it when I go out.
Mommy, Mommy, why are there tears in your eyes?
Baby, my sweet, sweet baby, it just doesn't work that way.
You can't take it off. You can't put it away.
The skin your in, is yours to wear, as well as the kink
that's in your hair.
I'm really sorry I can't change what other people say,
think or do.
The tears on my face are sorrow's water.
Sorrow for failing to prepare you yesterday...for today
and tomorrow.
It was my job to pass on our story, to fill your head with

the truth of our glory.
To give you strength to wear the skin you're in.
You can't take it off.   You can't put it away.
It's a part of you. Be proud of your skin, and the kink of
your hair.
It's a part of you, that's here to stay...and starting right
now, this very minute I'll tell you our history and why you
are in it...

Thousands of years ago on the shores of....

Lookin'

Are you the one?
Are you the one?
Are you the one?
Are you the one?

Are you the one whose gonna change what is into what will
be?
Are you the one who's gonna do the things that need to
be done, to make this world a better place?

Are you?
Cause I've been lookin' from time before time.

Are you the one?
Are you the one that's gonna find the cure to erase pain,
poverty, and diseases?

Are you?
Are you the one?

Are you the one that's gonna succeed against the odds, to
achieve all that can be?

Is that you?
Cause I'm still lookin', from now until time eternal.

Are you the one who will inspire all of us to rise even
higher, to do what's right just because it is?

Are you the one?

Is the one you?

Cause I'll never gonna stop lookin' or askin'.

Are you the one? Are you the one? Are you...

Grandma's Encouragement

Baby girl,
keep pressin on.
Don't let nothin hold you back,
for every problem that comes up
there's a plan of attack.
For every trouble that comes your way,
for every test,
each trial or tribulation.
You got the guts,
the grits, the determination.
You can overcome, when you keep
keeping on.
Nothin can stop you
Nothin can defeat you
Nothin can keep you
from becoming whatever
you choose.
So, baby girl,
Don't ever give up
Keep on tryin
Keep on striven
Keep on bein strong, keep on
Keeping on!
Baby girl!!!

It is a mask...

There was a time when all us (black folk)
knew about the mask we chose to wear
we understood the need for its protection
the need to keep hidden our true emotions from a sometimes
cruel and uncaring world
So we wore the mask, not to hide from ourselves...but to
protect ourselves from others.
It was a mask...
Now it seems many have forgotten that indeed it was only a
mask.
They've molded their features until they've become
permanent.
The mask of self-protection has become their mask of self-
destruction,
Causing them to fail to see the beauty in themselves and in
others.
Making it ok to be uncaring, unconcerned about anyone other
than one's self
The mask allows them to kill each other over anything with
anything
To destroy our communities, disrespect our elders, not value
other's lives
It was a mask...
    It can come off to reveal who and what we truly are
    to celebrate the greatness of our heritage
    it can come off and return our ability to build not tear down
                to respect
                to nurture
                to protect
                to love...to care

Understand...remember...think back....

                      It is a mask!

Take it off, unmold yourself.
        Reveal to the world your true self,
            the men and women we truly are.

Take off the mask, that grins, and lies, that hides your cheeks and shades your eyes...throw it off in our community, come from behind it.

It is a mask!...

Let the love that's in you radiate,
Let the true heritage of Africa's greatness spring forth.

Never forget our forefathers wore the mask to protect and ensure our futures.
Don't let their lives be lived in vain.

Do your part...
Unmask!

Life Quest

Write your life...the truth.
Write your life...simple as it is
Complex as it is.
Tell the story, minus all the fluff.
Don't try to glamorize
Don't try to make it up.
Don't try to force the words to come.
Just open up your soul, let your hidden feeling flow
from deep within.
Let them surface...expose them to the light.
Write your life...the truth.
Unafraid to be yourself,
unafraid to let your true feelings show,
unafraid to enjoy the feelings of liberation,
unafraid to enjoy the discovery of your free will.
Simply by picking up a pen,
and writing your life...the truth.
Telling of your passions, sharing your joy,
embracing your heartaches and your sorrows.
Seeking your own true path.
Deciding your own future,
unencumbered by false feelings, unedited, uncensored.
No longer over analyzed.
No more time spent trying to rationalize or
understand the reason(s) or the why(s).
Just the determination to
tell your story.
To write your life...the truth.

Congratulations, you have become a
part of the never-ending rhyme.
Thank you for taking the time to go on
my journey of rhythm and rhyme!!!
I hope you've enjoyed the ride.
My goal was to challenge, inspire,
encourage, and entertain.
My mission was to share with you my
thoughts and feelings.
My hope is that I've succeeded in
making you happy and sad...
         making you thoughtful
         making you mad
         making you think
         making you pause
         making you wonder
         making you question...
      but mostly making you think!

Thoughts and Notes of the Rhythms

Thoughts and Notes of the Rhythms

Thoughts and Notes of the Rhythms

Thoughts and Notes of the Rhythms

Thoughts and Notes of the Rhythms

Thoughts and Notes of the Rhythms

About the Author

Janet was born September 30th, 1954, in Wurtzburg, Germany. She is the 5th of 12 children born to Robert I. (deceased) and Christine Webb. Her early childhood was spent on various Army bases. In 1959, the family moved to Joliet, IL. Janet attended the public schools in Joliet, graduating from Joliet Township High School Central Campus in June 1972.

In August of 1972, Janet moved to Evanston to attend National College of Education, now National-Louis University. Upon graduating in 1976, she began her teaching career at Haven Middle School. In 1985, she moved to Evanston Township High School, where she currently teaches mathematics.

Janet has earned a BA and a MA in Education as well as a Certificate of Advanced Studies in Educational Leadership all from National-Louis University.

The Rhythm Ain't Gotta Rhyme is the first published volume of poetry written by Janet Webb.

Janet's love of writing poetry was inspired early in life. This inspiration can be attributed to her teacher, mentor and friend Mrs. Vivian Ward Penneymon.

Printed in the United States
42848LVS00006B/376-1008